Revenge of the Vegetarian

A Humorous Spin on the World of Vegetarianism

By Jim Tilberry

With Patricia Van Winkle

Table of Contents

Intro

"Revenge is a dish best served with mixed vegetables."

Socrates
413 B.C.

When I started writing this book some people asked me why I was doing it. They wondered if there weren't already enough books on vegetarianism. So why was I writing another one?

Well, there's an obvious answer. I needed the money.

But a secondary reason is that I wasn't satisfied with the information offered in other books. Where were the books that give hygienic advice on how to kiss a meat eater? Where were books telling vegetarians how to come out of the closet? Where were the books that had psychic interviews with famous dead vegetarians?

Where? Where? Where?

Well truthfully I didn't really look for books with these topics, but I assumed they would be hard to find. If they didn't show up on the first page of my Google search, frankly it was too much effort.

So I decided to write my own book which would cover the important topics missing from most vegetarian books.

Another question people asked me a lot was whether I had ever met Dr. Roscoe "Beanie" McBride. If you've never seen him on *Meet the Press* or that one episode of *COPS*, he is the colorful leader of the fledgling vegetarian political party, known as the *Vegocrats*.

I met Dr. McBride just one time in the mid-90's at an animal-rights fundraiser in Alexandria, Virginia. He was a congressman from Mississippi back then. We exchanged a few minutes of small talk. I remember his mentioning a fondness for Elvis Presley and Asian women with pink highlights, but not much more. Towards the end of the evening McBride became quite wasted and obnoxious. He was spouting off incoherent rants such as "Down with the meat-eating bourgeoisie" and "Ole McDonald was a sell-out." Years later I was surprised to see McBride rise to the top of his own political party. So I figured he was worth writing about, especially now that he's running for president.

A third question many people asked me was why I employed a psychic in writing this book. After all, I was never much interested in the spiritual world. So at first glance, it may seem like an odd collaboration.

Actually the reason I hired a psychic is because I don't hear well.

In the beginning I certainly didn't plan to have a chapter which would feature conversations with the spirits of Albert Einstein and Adolf Hitler. However one of my friends highly recommended

Patricia Van Winkle, telling me she was an excellent psychic. But I misheard him.

I thought he said she was an excellent *sidekick*. And who *couldn't* use an excellent sidekick? I wasn't exactly sure what the duties of a sidekick were, but at the time I was thinking light housework and foot massages.

So I called up Patricia Van Winkle and hired her, only to find out later that she had no interest in touching my feet or performing any of the other sidekick duties I had in mind. However, when we were about to part ways, she told me something interesting, something you don't hear every day.

She claimed as a psychic she could summon the spirits of any dead vegetarian I wanted to interview -- Einstein, Hitler, Gandhi, you name it. That sounded pretty cool to me, so I thought why not? Who *wouldn't* want to know what Hitler's favorite legume was? And of course, I was curious if Einstein was pissed that he didn't get to cash in on Einstein Bagels.

The vegetarian horoscope Patricia later created turned out to be a bonus, as was the section on animal communication with former carnivores.

In putting these pages together I also owe a lot to two gentlemen who enthusiastically helped me with this project.

My neighbor, Randy Buford, was a good sport in trying to go on a vegetarian diet after living nearly 40 years on bacon, burgers and bratwurst. I have reprinted Randy's food diary from his first week as a vegetarian. Sadly I suspect the cholesterol withdrawal he is experiencing will make it very difficult for Randy to ever be a stellar vegetarian.

I'd also like to acknowledge my research assistant, Sheldon Bumpus, for his help in putting together the Answers-to-Questions section and the V.Q. quiz on page 100. Hopefully his brief stint in jail will not sour his view of the importance of meaningful food-related experiments, even if they occasionally break the law.

Finally, I'd like to thank *you* for the wise decision of purchasing this book. Undoubtedly you will learn a lot from the following chapters.

Whether you're a meat eater, a vegetarian, or a meat eater pretending to be a vegetarian, there's something here for you. In fact, this could be the most educational book you'll ever read on vegetarianism.

But I'm also assuming you don't read much.

10 Great Reasons to Become a Vegetarian

There are a lot of wonderful benefits to being on a vegetarian diet. Of course, there are the obvious things such as improving your health, helping the environment, and getting fewer gravy stains. However, there are also many less heralded benefits to giving up meat.

Here are 10 great often-overlooked reasons to become a vegetarian.

1. **You can make people feel uncomfortable anytime you want**. This is a handy technique, especially if you ever find yourself stuck talking with a real bore at a party. Just mention that you're a vegetarian and that you think all meat eaters are scum. Then watch him quickly excuse himself to go talk to someone else.

2. **You get to choose the restaurant where you eat when out with friends.** If someone picks a restaurant you don't like, in your whiniest voice say "But it's not vegetarian-friendly! There's nothing I can eat there." The others in your group will relent and go with your choice. *Caveat: You may find that you're never invited out to dinner again by these same friends.*

3. **You always have a convenient excuse to explain your flatulence**. Just say something like "Sorry. It was that bean burrito I had for lunch. As you may know, I'm a vegetarian now." Everyone will sympathize and understand completely.

4. **Show off your vocabulary**. When discussing your diet, use veggie words like "vegan," "tempeh" and "seitan." Meat eaters will see you as unique and exotic. Then if you really want to impress them with how smart you are, throw around bigger words like "monounsaturated," "phytochemicals," and "isoflavones." Don't worry about learning their meanings. Just being able to pronounce them is impressive enough. Besides, no will ask their meanings for fear of looking stupid.

5. **Food fights are less greasy**. Generally speaking, vegetables aren't as slimy as meat. So your toss is more accurate when throwing Brussels sprouts and bananas over hurling meatballs or sausages. It's also less gross when you get hit.

6. **If you have no religion tell people you're a vegetarian.** Being a vegetarian can save you the embarrassment of not of having a practicing religion. If someone asks what you are just mumble the "veg" part of the word, so all they hear is "etarian." Nine times out of ten they won't be paying any attention and will just nod.

7. **It's easier to pick up women**. When you're at a bar or party, tell the woman you just met that you're a vegetarian because you care about animals.

If you're a man, watch her swoon because you're such a *sensitive guy*.

Or if you're a lesbian, watch her swoon because you're such a *sensitive gal*.

8. **Worry less about farm animals judging you**. Animals are very intuitive. Cows, pigs and chickens can be very judgmental in what they think about humans, especially meat eaters. However, because you're a vegetarian, next time you encounter a cow or a pig, or hold a chicken, there's less likelihood they will think you're a dirtbag.

9. **Make your new tattoo a conversation starter.** Instead of the usual skull-and-cross-bones tattoo, get a cauliflower-and-broccoli tattoo. Or get the popular tofu-in-a-heart tattoo. Granted it's not as intimidating if you find yourself at a biker bar, but it will be a great conversation piece at parties.

10. **Avoid a serious injury on Thanksgiving.** Every Thanksgiving all across America there are dozens of frozen-turkey accidents caused by people losing their grip and dropping the slippery bird. Carrying the humungous turkey from the car can be downright hazardous. Even removing it from the refrigerator is risky. A slight slip can result in a bruised foot, broken toe or even *death*. As a vegetarian you can safely excuse yourself from ever handling the big bird.

What You Can Eat on a Vegetarian Diet

One of the common myths about vegetarians is that their diets are boring and there's no variety. To that I say *baloney*! Or more appropriately, *soy baloney*.

As you can see from the food pyramid below there's a lot of variety in the vegetarian diet. The possibilities for different types of meals are endless, or six, whichever comes first.

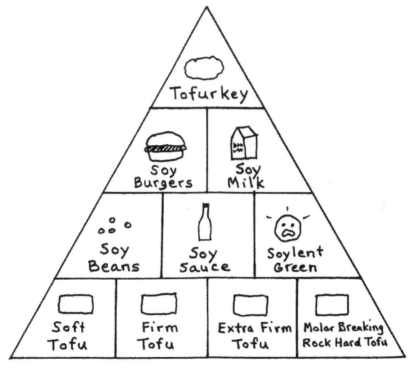

The Vegetarian Food Pyramid

Of course I'm just kidding about the vegetarian pyramid on the previous page. There's a lot more variety than just soy products.

However many meat eaters are under the huge misconception that there's nothing *great tasting* on a vegetarian diet. Nothing could be further from the truth. Just look at all of the mouth-watering food options below.

Salad
Fruit
Fruit Salad
Beans
Bean salad
Pickles
Pickle juice
Pickle salad
Fruit-bean-pickle salad
Broccoli
Water (*except the popular sirloin-flavored water*)
Seaweed
Algae
Jicama (*In Spanish means "big fat ugly potato"*)
Mustard
Broccoli
Acorns (*let them soak for a few weeks to soften*)
Rutabaga
Nutritional yeast
Cereal (*excludes Lucky Charms with Pork Pieces or Cocoa Krispies with Liver Bits*)
Tree bark (*great source of fiber!*)

Dandelions *(Load up in spring to freeze for later in the year)*
Houseplant leaves that have fallen off *(meal tip: try adding to your fruit-bean-pickle salad)*
Pine seeds
Pine nuts
Pinecones (*Be sure to floss afterwards!* ☺)
Wheat germ oil
Broccoli
Ice cubes
Fruit-bean-pickle-and-ice-cube salad

Angry Foods to Avoid
Hot Potato
Grapes of Wrath
Killer Tomatoes

Vegetarian vs. Meat Eater Diet

Vegetarians have an easier time with digestion than meat eaters. The reasons should be obvious when you compare their stomachs and digestive tracts. Vegetarian diets have a lot more fiber. No bones about it. Or horns or hooves.

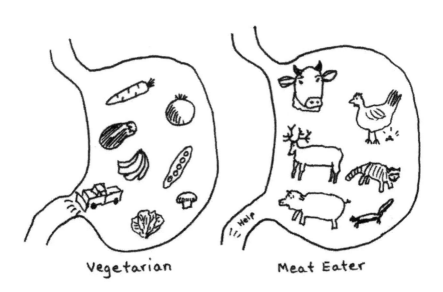

Vegetarian   Meat Eater

Veg Speak

Here are the 11 types of vegetarians

Vegan – Someone who does not eat or drink any animal products, wear any animal products, look at pictures of animals, watch television shows with animals on them, or dream about animals

Lacto Vegetarian – One who does not eat meat but will use dairy products such as milk, butter, and cheesehead hats

Ovo Vegetarian – One who doesn't eat animal products, with one eggception

Pesco Vegetarian – One who will seafood and eat it

Pesco Pollo Vegetarian – One who eats fish and chicken, and calls himself a vegetarian with a straight face

Octo Ovo Hojo Vegetarian – One who eats eight eggs a day, primarily at Howard Johnson's restaurants

Strict Vegetarian – One who doesn't let his daughter date until she is 25

White Meat & Bacon Vegetarian – One who has made the supreme sacrifice of giving up liver

Lacto Wacko Vegetarian – One who drinks 20 glasses of milk a day for no particular reason

Contrarian Vegetarian – One who is the opposite of what you'd expect: an old overweight Republican who smokes

Breathatarian Vegetarian – A level 10 vegan, one who consumes only air and filtered water for sustenance

Removing the Meat of the Language

There are many "meat" references and sayings in American English vernacular. Although not necessarily intended to be insensitive, many of these expressions are in fact offensive to vegetarians.

Dr. Roscoe "Beanie" McBride has vowed to change parts of the English language which he considers hurtful to animals and vegetarians.

When he served as a congressman from Mississippi, McBride put a bill before the House which would have legally removed many politically-incorrect sayings, replacing them with ones that are more veggie-friendly.

The bill was soundly voted down 434 to 1. Unfazed, McBride promises to champion the cause of making English a meat-free language.

Here are a few of the words and expressions he advocates changing:

Current expression
"Chopped liver" (i.e. What am I, chopped liver?)

Would change to:
"Chopped broccoli" (i.e. Why did you invite *him* to help you install your new juicer? What am I, chopped broccoli?)

Current expression
"Meat of the matter"

Would change to:
"Tofu of the topic" (i.e. Finally after a long opening to his speech, Bernie got down to the tofu of the topic.)

Current expression
"Bringing home the bacon"

Would change to:
"Bringing home the textured-soy-and-wheat-protein strips." (i.e. Tom stays home with the kids, while Sally is out bringing home the textured-soy-and-wheat-protein strips.)

Current expression
"Cooked goose"

Would change to:
"Toasted tofurkey" (i.e. He's in big trouble. His tofurkey is toasted.)

Coming Out

Many vegetarians live secret lives. Out of shame or fear, they hide their dietary lifestyle from others. It's easy to understand why.

When vegetarians come out of the closet they open themselves up to potential teasing and even bullying by their carnivore friends. It can be a very humiliating time for the individual whose "unconventional" eating habits have been exposed to others.

However it can also feel very liberating to the vegetarian since he no longer has to hide his secret. He can at last be out in the open about his lifestyle. Ultimately there is a great sense of relief. With the secret revealed, a weight has been lifted off his shoulders.

Telling Mom and Dad

The first step in this process of coming out is usually telling one's family. A vegetarian must summon a lot of courage to tell his parents and other family members about his vegetarian habits. This is a difficult and traumatic experience for everyone involved.

Parents are often devastated by the news. They likely will be unsupportive of their adult child's diet. In fact, at first the parents may even be in denial. They'll try to reason with the child. They'll attempt various arguments about why this "vegetarian lunacy" won't last.

"You're just going through a phase."

"A lot people like to experiment with these things at your age."

"We're not worried. You'll come to your senses eventually and start eating meat again."

But he'll tell them that this isn't just a phase. The vegetarian lifestyle is not just a choice. It's who he is. It's the way he was born. He'll tell his parents that for years he fought the feelings that he'd like to be a vegetarian. However, the feelings were just too strong to overcome. And finally he had come to terms with who he is.

Then the parents will likely get angry and blame each other.

The father will blame the mother "Helen, it's all your fault. You forced him to eat his vegetables growing up. If you had just let him walk away from the dinner table without finishing his peas everything would be OK. He wouldn't be so messed up today. He'd be like every other normal kid in America -- he *never* would have learned to like his veggies."

Then the mother will get defensive and lash back at the father, "My fault!? You're kidding me?!? No, it's all *your* fault he turned out this way. When he was a boy, you were a terrible role model. You didn't make him help you when you were grilling steaks on the barbeque. He never learned to appreciate the satisfaction of cooking a juicy grade-A tenderloin."

At this point the child will interrupt explaining it's nobody's fault. He'll try to reassure the parents that this really doesn't change things between him and them. It just means that family dinners and get-togethers around the holidays may be a little awkward at first. But eventually everything will get back to normal.

But the mention of holidays only makes the mother hysterical. She will break down sobbing "But what about Thanksgiving?!? What about the turkey?!? What will you eat? What *will* you eat? You're so *skinny* already!"

As the mother continues her sobbing, the father will chime in "It's that radical, good-for-nothing friend of yours, Chris Barnes, isn't it? I'll bet Chris talked you into this unorthodox lifestyle choice."

As the mother wipes away the tears, she'll turn to the child, and in a soft caring voice say "Maybe we can have Mr. Harrison, the butcher at our grocery store, talk to you. He'll explain that it's unnatural to not eat meat. Honey, would you be willing to have a sit-down with Mr. Harrison?"

Groaning in frustration, the adult child will explain that it won't do any good. Nothing can change his mind.

In desperation, the parents will then try other manipulative ploys to get him to resume eating meat. They'll offer him $1000 to give up vegetables. They'll agree to pay for therapy. They'll even threaten to send him to a meat-and-potatoes boot camp.

When nothing apparently works in changing the mind of the child, the mother and father will argue the case that the vegetarian lifestyle is *immoral*. "What about the poor pig farmers and chicken farmers?" the mother will plead, then adding "How would they survive if everybody went on a cockamamie vegetarian diet?"

The father will state that "not eating meat is just plain "un-American." As an afterthought he'll add "You know, I think *Hitler* was a vegetarian."

The discussions and arguments will continue for minutes, then hours, then days. There will be lots of yelling. There will be more crying. There will be many bathroom breaks.

Eventually the parents will come to accept their child for who he is. Even the family dog, a lifetime carnivore, will be accepting. The family cat, however, will remain distrusting and aloof.

At the culmination of this family meeting, several days later, there will be a group hug. Everyone will profess their unconditional love for each other. And they will order in a vegetarian pizza.

Dead Vegetarians
Speak Beyond the Grave

To help us communicate with the spirits of past vegetarians, we hired psychic **Patricia Van Winkle**. She telepathically communicated with famous dead vegetarians on their thoughts about being vegetarian and what experiences stand out in their memories.

Patricia Van Winkle is a qualified
psychic, numerologist and
Jiffy Lube technician.

Ben Franklin

Patricia Van Winkle: What was it like being a vegetarian in the eighteenth century?

Ben Franklin: The founding fathers used to tease me about being vegetarian. In fact, George Washington could be a real a-hole about it. He used to say that *"vegetarian* is an old Indian word for *lousy hunter."* Good one, George. I think that joke goes back to the Pilgrims. Anyway being a vegetarian in the eighteenth century was definitely harder than it is now. Back then we didn't have Whole Foods, veggie burgers or even soy milk. But it was worth it. It clearly boosted my social life. Having a diet that supported animal rights really impressed the ladies. That and having my picture on a hundred-dollar bill.

Thomas Edison

Patricia Van Winkle: Did you have any inventions for vegetarians?

Thomas Edison: Few people are aware that I was the original inventor of the Vegomatic blender. As I recall, I completed inventing the damn thing, caught the flu, and forgot to file a patent. So 70 years later some schmuck got credit for it and went on to make millions. To this day it irks me to hear people mention my breakthrough inventions: the light bulb, motion-picture camera, phonograph, etc… while leaving out two of my greatest inventions, the Vegomatic and rubber vomit.

Mahatma Gandhi

Patricia Van Winkle: I understand you were a passionate vegetarian.

Mahatma Gandhi: Being an Indian and vegetarian is not a big a deal. There must be a gazillion of us. Of course most of us have a loving respect for all animals. And many of us believe in reincarnation. You never know -- that cow I see on the street could have been my Grandma Nana in another lifetime. So when I saw someone eating meat, I'd get extremely pissed off and just want to punch their lights out. Then I'd tell myself "Chill, Mohandas. You're supposed to be a non-violent pacifist."

Van Winkle: Were you ever tempted to eat meat?

Gandhi: I admit it. Every now and then I'd think to myself "I wonder what a Big Mac tastes like?" Then presto, the image of Grandma Nana mysteriously appeared in my head. That's freaky enough, but she always had a cowbell on her neck.

Socrates

Patricia Van Winkle: How did you get started on a vegetarian diet?

Socrates: Does the man choose a diet or does a diet choose the man?

Van Winkle: Hmm. . . OK. So you say that people are closely linked to vegetables. Can you elaborate?

Socrates: A human *being* in reality is just a human *bean*.

Van Winkle: I'm not quite following you. How so?

Socrates: If you take away its leg, a legume is just u and me.

Van Winkle: Alright. I think I see where you're going with that. And how would you say a vegetarian diet affected you?

Socrates: If you eat a meal of meat, you will be happy for 30 *minutes*. If you eat a meal of vegetables you will be happy for 30 *years*. *(Pause)* Unless some shithead gives you hemlock and tells you it's a V8.

Susan B. Anthony

Patrica Van Winkle: It's an honor to interview you. You've always been one of my heroines, a real trailblazer.

Susan B. Anthony: Oh, stop sucking up.

Van Winkle: I'm sorry. I didn't mean to. But the truth is, I just think you're wonderful.

Anthony: Now you're making me gag.

Van Winkle: I apologize. You know, one thing I was wondering – as the first feminist, did you ever burn your bra?

Anthony: Do your homework. The bra wasn't even invented when I was alive. But I did burn my corset once.

Van Winkle: A corset burning, huh? That's quite an act of rebelliousness.

Anthony: No, I stood too close to a wood stove.

Van Winkle: I see. So you were a suffragist, a temperance worker, an abolitionist, a labor activist, and a vegetarian.

Anthony: What's your question?

Van Winkle: Why didn't that dollar coin ever catch on?

Anthony: This interview is over.

Albert Einstein

Patrica Van Winkle: As I understand it, you weren't exactly an "Einstein" in school.

Albert Einstein: Yeah, it's embarrassing, but I used to be as dumb as a doorknob. I think eating meat was clogging my arteries and blocking the flow of blood to my brain.
Then I went vegetarian. I became infinitely sharper when I switched from bratwurst to broccoli.

Van Winkle: So becoming a vegetarian made you a brainiac?

Einstein: Correct.

Van Winkle: Isn't your brain in a museum or science lab or something?

Einstein: I really don't know. My brain keeps getting stolen, so I can never keep track of where it is.

Van Winkle: Wasn't it on eBay last year?

Einstein: Yes. Occasionally it shows up in weird places.

Van Winkle: And when was the last time you remember seeing your brain?

Einstein: It was a contestant on *Celebrity Apprentice*.

Ed Begley Jr.

Patrica Van Winkle: So how is heaven?

Ed Begley Jr: What are you talking about?

Van Winkle: I was just wondering if you've had a chance to talk with other famous vegetarians since you passed away. Maybe Steve Jobs?

Begley: Are you kidding? I'm not dead.

Van Winkle: You're not?

Begley: No.

Van Winkle: *(Pause)* Well this is awkward.

Begley: I'm very much alive. Why would you think I was dead?

Van Winkle: Well, I just haven't seen your name in a long time. *St. Elsewhere* was like a million years ago. I just assumed.

Begley: I've been very busy with a lot of environmental work. Like right now I'm designing a urine-powered toaster. *(Pause)* You could've just done a quick Google search of my name, instead of assuming I'd died.

Van Winkle: I uh. . . um. . . My phone is ringing. I've got to go.

Adolf Hitler

Patrica Van Winkle: First, I have to ask you if you have any regrets about your role in history.

Adolf Hitler: In hindsight, starting WW II was not my best idea ever. I blame my parents for my passive-aggressive personality. I obviously had some issues, and took out my frustrations on Europe. Sorry. My bad.

Van Winkle: So I was surprised to learn that you were a vegetarian.

Hitler: Goebbels got me into the diet, said it would help get me regular. And it worked. It certainly got me moving, if you know what I mean. Then when Eva and I were stuck in the bunker there were absolutely no fresh fruits or vegetables. None at all. Just a bunch of tuna cans, crackers and Cheez Whiz. So I was horribly constipated, which made me not a nice person. Sure, I was also bummed that we were getting our Nazi butts kicked. But not getting my daily veggies made life in the bunker a real hell.

Van Winkle: Speaking of hell, how is it?

Hitler: Tolerable. It's a dry heat.

Dr. Benjamin Spock

Patrica Van Winkle: So do you miss your days on *Star Trek*?

Dr. Benjamin Spock: What?

Van Winkle: I was just making a joke. Never mind.

Spock: I don't get it.

Van Winkle: Moving on. Did you advocate vegetarianism for babies?

Spock: Yes, I thought the earlier a child became a vegetarian the healthier he would be in life.

Van Winkle: Didn't you write a book on the subject?

Spock: Yes, I did write a book. It was titled "What to Feed the Little Bastard." But it didn't sell well.

Van Winkle: A provocative title.

Spock: Yeah, I was a little burned out at the time.

Leonardo da Vinci

Patricia Van Winkle: I just had a psychic communication with Thomas Edison. He told me to say "hi" to the world's *second* greatest inventor.

Leonardo da Vinci: Funny man, that Edison. Was he bitching about the Vegomatic again? What a bambino! You know how many inventions I had knocked off? Have you heard of the *helicopter*? Don't even get me started on the unauthorized use of my last name for book and movie titles.

Van Winkle: Hmm. . . Okay, I won't. So were you a Renaissance man with vegetarian cooking?

da Vinci: Oh yes. True story -- you know how I got Mona Lisa to work for me? I told her I'd make her my famous vegetarian lasagna if she would pose. But as it turned out, I was out of pasta, so I ended up giving her a stale loaf of bread to go. Mama mia, was she pissed! She never posed for me again. Unfortunately I hadn't painted her smile yet. So finishing the portrait, I used the smile of my mailman, Luigi.

Jesus Christ

Patricia Van Winkle: What was your childhood like?

Jesus Christ: When growing up I got razzed a lot for being the son of God. My friends loved to tease me for who my father was. But it only got worse when I became a vegetarian. Being the son of God *and* a vegetarian was like a double whammy in ancient Judea. The disciples used to call me the "stereotypical hippie," with my long hair, beard, and vegetarian diet.

Van Winkle: So did you stick with a meatless diet to the very end?

Jesus: Almost. During the Last Supper, when I was out back taking a leak, Judas secretly put goat meat in my vegetable bowl. What a dick. I never could trust that dude. Anyway I had stomach problems all the next day. Needless to say, my indigestion made it a bad day. Not to mention the crucifixion thing.

Quitting Meat

One of the hardest things to do when becoming a vegetarian is kicking the meat-eating habit. Why is it so hard? And why do so many new vegetarians give up and go back to eating meat? Here are just a few of the reasons.

Lingering Addiction

Meat-eater brains are hard-wired to order double bacon cheeseburgers, make a beeline to the pork section of the grocery, and pick up beef sticks when stopping at 7-Eleven. These powerful addictions take time to overcome.

Unwelcome Weight Change

Meat eaters who become vegetarians usually lose weight. A smaller body size conflicts with the big-body image meat eaters are used to. It causes confusion. Most meat eaters are used to carrying around excess pounds, and as a vegetarian they feel like "less of a person."

Irritability

New vegetarians become frustrated when grocery shopping because they have a hard time finding all of the new healthy foods they used to avoid like the plague. They are often heard muttering curses like "Where the hell is the produce section?" "How come tofu isn't with the canned vegetables?" and "Why is almond milk not *next to* the Almond Joys?"

Withdrawal Symptoms

New vegetarians often experience strange physical changes. These could include better circulation, lower blood pressure, lower cholesterol and more energy. These changes are all very unsettling. They have a hard time reconciling their new body with their previous body. Some may even fear their body has been taken over by an alien body snatcher.

With all of these factors working against the new vegetarian, it obviously takes a lot of willpower to give up meat. That's why many people can't succeed on their own. They need help. Fortunately there are several scientifically proven techniques and aids to help you quit.

Eliminate Temptation

Before you start your meat-free diet, it's important to get rid of meat reminders in your home that could trigger cravings. Tear up that big poster of the Hooters girl in your bedroom. Throw out your discount coupons for Burger King. And delete the Omaha Steaks 800 # from your speed dial.

Once you eliminate all household reminders of your previous meat-consuming habit, you're ready to begin. Here are six great techniques to help you quit meat and be meat-free for life.

The Meat Patch

Meat patches release measured doses of simulated beef, chicken or pork into your bloodstream to curb your meat cravings. They're usually the equivalent of an 8-ounce steak filet or two pork chops over eight hours. For heavy meat eaters trying to kick the habit, several patches can be used at once on different body parts. Over time as your cravings become less frequent, you can switch to lower-dose patches which release smaller amounts of "meat" into your system, about the equivalent of one chicken nugget over 24 hours.

Pro: As long as you wear the patches under your clothes, no one will know.

Con: Forgetting you have a meat patch stuck on your rear end, could be an embarrassment when showering at the health club.

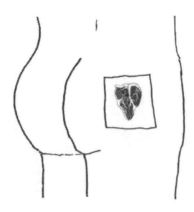

Other Meat-Delivery Systems

In addition to the patch there are other meat-delivery systems that have become available in recent years either over the counter or through a doctor's prescription.

Meat-flavored gum helps diminish cravings as you try to stay meat-free. Gum flavors such as *Beef Bubble*, *Liver-licious*, and *Juicy Pork* are quite popular and available in drugstores.

Lozenges (i.e. beef-stew flavored *Stew-crets*), nasal spray (i.e. *Bacon Mist*) and water (i.e. *Aqua Pepperoni*) also get simulated meat into your body to diminish your urge to chow down on the real thing.

Aversion Therapy

If every time you see, smell, or taste meat, you associate something unpleasant which makes you physically sick, then you are much less likely to resume the habit. That is the principle behind *aversion therapy*. Here are three common techniques used by clinicians to administer meat-aversion therapy.

1. While eating one's favorite hamburger, the voice of Fran Drescher is played into the subject's headphones.

2. While snacking on a bucket of KFC, the subject is strapped into a chair and forced to watch an Adam Sandler movie.

3. The subject is forced to eat a ham sandwich, while having a one-on-one lunch with Newt Gingrich.

After going through any of the above techniques the subjects typically have such a horrible association with the meat-eating experience that they become nauseated at even the thought of meat.

Pro: After you endure your aversion-therapy session, everything else you experience in life will seem like a picnic.

Con: You must endure several God-awful minutes which could scar you for life.

Hypnosis

Once considered out of the mainstream of modern science, hypnosis is now an accepted technique for behavior modification. A licensed hypnotist will put you in a deep trance and have you visualize yourself as an herbivore, such as a cow, horse, or sheep. You will come out of your trance refreshed and ready to go vegetarian.

Pro: Hypnosis can be very effective for quickly eliminating meat-eating urges.

Con: Your neighbors might notice you on all fours, grazing on your front lawn.

Subliminal CDs

Subliminal messages are very effective for planting thoughts at a subconscious level. When receiving a subliminal message a person has a strong impulse to do something, but doesn't know why.

There are several meat-quitting subliminal CDs on the market which play soothing music. Imbedded in the music, and inaudible to the human ear, are several powerful messages which motivate people to give up meat and become vegetarian.

Here's a short example from one of the CDs, "Subliminal Meat-Quitting Messages -- For Losers Who Can't Quit On Their Own." Again the messages cannot be heard audibly, but they do register at the subconscious level.

♫♫♪♪♫♫♪♫ Funny Clown is a Vegetarian ♫♪♫♫♪♫

♫♫♪♪♫♫ Scary Clown is a Meat Eater ♫♫♫♫ ♫♫♫♫♫♪

♪♫♫♪♫♫ Cool Aunt eats Veggies ♪♫♫♫♫♪♫♪

♫♫♫♪♪♫♫ Creepy Uncle eats Meat ♫♫♫♫♪♪♫♪♫♫♫

♫♪♫♫♫♪♪♫♫♫♫♪♪ Tofu with Hot Sex ♫♫♫♫♫♪♪♫♫♫♫♪♫♪

♫♫♫♪♪♫♫ Bacon with Naked Grandma ♫♫♪♫♫♫♪♫

Pro: Playing subliminal message CDs takes little effort on your part.

Con: Without understanding why, at times you might find yourself singing some very weird lyrics.

Acupuncture

Getting needles stuck in various weird parts of your body may not be your cup of tea. But if being some Asian doc's pin cushion for the day will help you quit meat, it's worth a try. The theory is that acupuncture points are targeted to both stimulate your love of the salad bar while suppressing your urge to scarf down a Big Mac.

Pro: Acupuncture is cool and you can brag to your friends about it. Afterward if your kids are bored they can play *connect the dots* with the holes.

Con: For the next few hours you'll need to avoid drinking beverages or you'll be spurting like a lawn sprinkler.

Answers to Questions from Vegetarians

Q. My husband is a meat eater and I'm a vegetarian. We're expecting our first child in a few months. I've heard that the vegetarian gene is recessive. Does that mean that our baby will automatically be a meat eater?

Sarah K.

A. In mixed marriages, like yours, where one parent is a meat eater and the other is a vegetarian, your meat-eating and meat-repelling genes are combined in your offspring. Your baby will be a semi-vegetarian.

Q. I'm concerned that if I ever have an accident and need a blood transfusion, I might be given blood from a meat eater. When admitted into a hospital, is there any way to ensure that I only get vegetarian blood?

Donald R.

A. Unfortunately not. Hospitals do not make an effort to keep meat eaters' blood separate from vegetarians' blood. That is why after surgery many vegetarians crave bacon cheeseburgers.

Q. I eat a lot of meat, yet no one ever sees me eating meat. In other words, I eat meat in the privacy of my own kitchen. Usually it's a salami-and-pickle sandwich late at night or early in the morning when no one else is around. Since no one ever sees me eating meat, am I *technically* a vegetarian?

Betsy W.

A. This is an excellent question. It's reminiscent of the old conundrum, if a tree falls in the forest but no one hears it, does it still make a sound? If you eat meat, but no one witnesses it, are you therefore a vegetarian? This is a profound question that could be argued by philosophers for ages to come. There is no right or wrong answer.

Q. I've been a vegetarian for a couple of years, but I'm interested in going all the way and becoming a vegan. I noticed that vegans tend to have more tattoos than regular vegetarians. I currently have just two tattoos in discrete places (lower back and ankle). Will I need to get more tattoos to become a vegan?

Karen M.

A. It depends. Some communities have unwritten rules about the number of tattoos required to become a vegan. Other places are less strict in their standards. Generally speaking, in most communities you will need at least three visible tattoos to become a vegan. However to be fully accepted among other vegans, it's advised to display at least five visible tattoos. These tats could be on your upper arms, forearms or neck. Nose, lip or eyebrow piercings would also help you fit in.

Q. I stopped eating meat about six weeks ago. Honestly I was surprised at how easy it was to become a vegetarian and how delicious most of the food is. My new diet consists mainly of sugar cookies, potato chips, coconut cream pie, glazed donuts, cheese puffs, and the occasional beer. However, I was wondering if my diet is balanced enough.   I heard that it's important to also get "greens" in the diet. Can you recommend any?

Courtney F.

A. First of all, congratulations on becoming a vegetarian! You have taken a big step toward better health, more energy and a longer life. And yes you're right – "greens" can make your meals better balanced. Try adding shamrock shakes to your diet.

Q. Recently I went to a big reunion of my wife's extended family. I happened to overhear my wife's 95-year old great aunt comment on how she believes there's nothing wrong with eating meat. So I dumped a big bowl of guacamole dip on her head. Was that wrong of me to do that?

William B.

A. Yes, that was completely wrong. You wasted some perfectly good guacamole. You would have been wiser to have dumped some type of meat casserole on her head.

Q. I'm 75 years old and went in for my annual checkup recently. While there, I was stunned that my doctor recommended that I should try juicing. She said it would give me better nutrition and improve my health. Isn't juicing illegal? I'm not a professional athlete. And I don't really want huge muscles and a tiny scrotum. Should I report her to the AMA?

Stephen H.

A. Yes, your doctor is obviously a renegade. You should report her immediately.

Q. In the last few months I've been drinking a lot of rice milk. Recently I read online that too much rice milk in your diet could turn you gay. Is this true? Also I've noticed I've been saying the word "legume" in conversations more often.

Paul G.

A. I think you've answered your own question.

Q. In the last couple of months I've attended a few vegetarian meet-ups held at restaurants here in Chicago. I'm new to this group and don't know a lot of the members. I'm also very shy and have had a hard time talking to new people. Usually I start conversations with these two questions: "How long have you been a vegetarian?" and "What made you decide to stop eating meat?" However after they answer these questions, the conversations often fizzle out and become awkward. Can you suggest interesting topics, or perhaps more questions I can ask when talking to someone new?

Michael P.

A. Here are three thought-provoking questions you can use at any vegetarian social function when you meet someone for the very first time:

1. Which came first -- vegetarian chicken or vegetarian eggs?

2. If everyone at this gathering is vegetarian, why do they call it a *meat*-up?

3. What color underwear do you have on?

After asking these questions, you'll have no trouble keeping the conversation flowing. You'll come across as smart, clever, and curious.

Q. After the football team had a big win, a lot of us went out to celebrate at a nearby restaurant. Some of the players were sitting at my table and started teasing me for being a vegetarian. One called me "Boca Burger Breath" and another one actually threatened me, telling the others "Let's give Mr. Veggie a wedgie." It was very uncomfortable and humiliating for me. I got very emotional and almost cried. This is what I want to know, isn't it horribly rude for Pee Wee football players to talk to their coach this way?

Tom V.

A. Dude, you need to cut back on the rice milk.

Q. A while ago I heard something about vegans needing B-12s. I can't remember the details. Can you shed some light on this?

Julie E.

A. You're probably thinking of B-52s. And yes, it's good for vegans and all vegetarians to listen to this cool band from Athens, Georgia. Their hit song "Rock Lobster" is virtually an anthem for the rights of all sea animals.

Q. My boyfriend eats meat and I don't. Often we go out to dinner and share a whole pizza, half meat and half veggie. My half of the pizza has black olives, mushrooms and green peppers. His half always has pepperoni, sausage, and Canadian bacon. My boyfriend eats fast and carelessly, often grabbing a slice from my side of the pizza by mistake. This makes me feel frustrated because I'm shortchanged. Since I don't eat meat, I can't compensate by taking one of his slices. Should I break up with him?

Kristi C.

A. No, that would be an extreme over reaction. I recommend the next time you catch him reaching for one of your slices that you stab his hand hard with your fork. He will get the message.

Q. I just started a vegetarian diet ten days ago and it's been hard. In this short time I have had a recurring dream where I'm chasing a huge McDonald's McRib sandwich. I chase it for quite awhile until it disappears off a cliff. I come up to the edge of the cliff and look down to see a huge vat full of Wendy's chili. Don't ask me how I know it's Wendy's chili, I just know. Then I feel strangely compelled to dive into the chili. When I rise to the surface, there's a giant Colonel Sanders there looking down into the bowl of chili. He doesn't scare me. In fact, even though I'm straight, I feel very attracted to him and compelled to swim toward him. What does this dream mean?

Charles D.

A. At some point, every vegetarian has this exact same dream. In fact, I had it twice last week. It just means you're not getting enough sex.

Q. I've read that Beanie McBride is running for president. Isn't he a bit of a nutjob?

Zach N.

A. Many people have called Vegocratic candidate Dr. Roscoe "Beanie" McBride eccentric. Certainly many of his ideas push the envelope on vegetarian rights. For example, not only does he want the word "meat" expunged from the English language, he also wants to make it illegal to use its homonym, "meet." Since "meet" sounds just like "meat," he considers it equally offensive to Vegetarian-Americans. The consequences of a ban of these two words would be far-reaching. For example, the singer/actor Meat Loaf would legally be required to change his name to "Veggie Loaf." A lot of movie and book titles would have to be changed too. "Meet the Fockers" would be re-titled "Become Acquainted with the Fockers." Even "meetings" would need to be renamed either "businesslike get-togethers" or "conference-room snoozefests." Despite the controversy of his proposals, many vegetarians appreciate the effort McBride is making to push for a meatless (and "meet-less") society.

Q. I've heard that Quorn is a good source of protein. Isn't Quorn the Islamic bible? And if I eat it, won't Muslims get upset?

Jerome T.

A. You're thinking of the Quran. And yes, it is high in protein. Just eat it discretely and certainly not while traveling in Arab countries.

Q. Last week I was at a dinner party and took an hors d'oeuvre off a platter, thinking it was vegetarian. As I was chewing I realized to my horror that it had meat in it. Then I was paralyzed with fear, unsure of what to do. I was uncertain whether to swallow, or spit it out into a napkin, and risk being embarrassed in front of other dinner-party guests. I ended up swallowing, but it was disgusting. If this ever happens again, what should I do?

Linda W.

A. The solution is really quite simple. If you start chewing something at a social function and realize it has meat in it, pretend you're choking. Make a bug-eyed look, hold your breath, groan loudly, flail your arms, and then repeatedly point to your throat. Most certainly one of the party guests will go behind you and administer the Heimlich maneuver. Then just spit out the chewed meaty glob. Try to aim so it doesn't hit another guest in the face. Then thank the person who performed the Heimlich for saving your life. No one will care that you just spat a gross piece of chewed meat. Party guests will be relieved that you're all right and probably give you more attention and sympathy for the rest of the evening.

Q. Since I started eating a lot more vegetables, I've been having some flatulence. This has caused me a great deal of embarrassment. Most recently I broke wind while giving the eulogy at my brother's funeral, which was quite humiliating. Is it common to experience gas when eating lots of vegetables?

Edith P.

A. Thank you for your letter. I showed it to my research assistant, Sheldon, and we both got a big kick out of it. In fact, Sheldon was laughing so hard, he spilled his beer all over his pants. That was almost as funny as your letter. Anyway, in answer to your question, I've never heard of anyone getting gas from eating too many vegetables. So it must be very unusual. Just try to stay away from other people unless you're in noisy well-ventilated areas. And Edith, thanks again for your letter. It was quite entertaining. Oh by the way, my condolences for the loss of your brother.

Psycho Vegetarian

The Dark Side of Vegetarian Culture

It's no secret that many meat eaters are leery of vegetarians. And for good reason. Vegetarians display several peculiar behaviors to say the least. The very fact that they don't eat meat is considered pretty darn weird by meat eaters. However there are other characteristics that non-vegetarians find even scarier. Here's a list of some of those frightening traits.

Tempeh Tantrums

Vegetarians are possessive about their tempeh, a strange food-like substance. And they get upset if it's missing. Beware the vegetarian who loses his tempeh.

Seitan Worship

Some vegetarians love seitan to the point of fanaticism. But don't let yourself get caught under the spell of this meat substitute just because it tastes good and is very healthy. It must be too good to be true. Run from the temptation.

Tofu Fungus

A disturbing trait among some vegetarians is that they'll keep open tofu in the refrigerator long past the expiration date – until it grows fur like a Chia Pet.

Miso Cool Syndrome

Pronounced "Me So Cool," this syndrome reflects an arrogant attitude among many vegetarians that they're better than you because they know words like *tempeh*, *seitan,* and *miso* and you don't.

Nutty Obsessions

Many vegetarians have an over-the-top fondness for nuts, and I'm not talking about those wacky and lovable Republican presidential candidates.

Converted Carnivores

The revealing stories of three creatures who gave up eating meat

We hired **Patricia Van Winkle** to telepathically interview some formerly-carnivorous animals who converted to vegetarianism. Ms. Van Winkle interviewed a dozen different animals who made the change to a meatless diet. Here are the interviews with three of the creatures.

Patricia Van Winkle is a
skilled animal communicator,
palm reader and
amateur pole-vaulter.

Smokey

Patricia Van Winkle: So are all cats curious?

Smokey: *That's* your opening question!? Are all cats curious!? What, did you go to the Chris Farley School of Journalism?

Van Winkle: I just wanted to start with some sort of icebreaker.

Smokey: (*Thinking to self:* What a doofus.)

Van Winkle: I can hear all your thoughts.

Smokey: Crap. Sorry dude.

Van Winkle: Ugh. Actually, I'm a woman. So why did you give up meat? It's just weird because cats are natural carnivores.

Smokey: Listen, being fat ain't fun. *You* certainly know what I'm talking about. I'm plump as a beach ball. My alley-cat pals call me "Tubby Tabby." And I've been too slow to catch a friggin' mouse for over a year. It sucks man. . . I mean lady.

Van Winkle: So I take it you decided to become a vegetarian to shed a few pounds?

Smokey: Figured that out all by yourself, Sherlock? Yes, being vegetarian will help me lose the LBs to get back my street cred.

Van Winkle: OK. Fortunately we're done here.

Smokey: So you're really not a dude?

Van Winkle: It's been a lot of fun. But I need to go now.

Billy

Patricia Van Winkle: So as a vegetarian you've given up eating insects?

Billy: It wasn't that hard. I used to eat every moth and ladybug I could lure in to my web. But like eating at the same restaurant every day of your life, I started to get a little bored with the menu. Plus, let's face it, eating bugs is just plain gross.

Van Winkle: Really? Even for a spider?

Billy: Hell yeah. It's like being on one of those disgusting eating segments of *Fear Factor* every single day, day after day. Yuck.

Van Winkle: I had no idea. Have you noticed any benefits to going veggie?

Billy: Since I began phasing out of creepy crawlers and adding more fruit and vegetables to my meals I've been more regular. Pooping used to be a pain, now it's a pleasure. . . . Gee, I hope that didn't sound too crude?

Van Winkle: Don't worry about it. Any other noticeable benefits?

Billy: I no longer have horsefly breath.

Margaret

Patricia Van Winkle: I appreciate you taking the time.

Margaret: No problem. I *love* the publicity. Just be sure to tell me when this will be on TV.

Van Winkle: Actually it's for a book. So anyway, it's hard to believe that a shark is really a vegetarian.

Margaret: Technically I'm now a *pesco* vegetarian. It wasn't really that hard to convert. My diet had always been about 99% seafood anyway. The only exception would be the occasional disoriented scuba diver.

Van Winkle: So why did you give up eating humans?

Margaret: It was a matter of improving my digestion. Quite often I would gulp down a scuba diver, oxygen tank and all. Ugh. Then I would have gas for several days. And it's hard for me to sneak up on my prey when there's constant stream of bubbles coming out of my ass.

Van Winkle: Interesting. Well, thank you.

Margaret: So this won't be on TV?

Van Winkle: No.

Margaret: Any chance you can get me on *Shark Tank*?

Van Winkle: It's really not that type of show.

Respect My Tofu

A staple of many vegetarian diets is a food called "Tofu," which should not be confused with the Asian "Toe Flu."

Tofu is made by coagulating soy milk. I don't know what that means, but it sounds boring, which makes sense since tofu by itself is pretty humdrum. It resembles plumbers' putty in consistency, but without the great taste. In fact, there's really no flavor at all.

Tofu is like a bed mattress. It has a rectangular shape. It comes in soft, firm and extra firm. And by itself, it's not terribly interesting. However, that's where the similarities end.

You probably wouldn't want to have sex on a big slab of tofu. Unless you're into that kind of thing. And if you are, I'm not judging you.

Even if it's not great for sleeping or having sex on, tofu is a very versatile food. It's quite high in protein, so it's a worthy meat substitute for stir fries, pasta dishes, or a Lady Gaga costume.

Unfortunately tofu doesn't get much respect from non-vegetarians. In fact, many meat eaters like to mock it, probably because the name tofu sounds more like a cartoon mouse than a real food. At one time, I even considered calling this book, "Don't Laugh at My Tofu." Then I learned that in certain Native American languages, tofu means *penis*.

A close cousin to tofu is something called "tofurkey," which for many vegetarians replaces turkey as the go-to food for Thanksgiving.

After Thanksgiving, vegetarians feast on tofurkey leftovers which are creatively used to make many interesting meals such as tofurkey sandwiches, tofurkey soup and tofurkey milkshakes.

As a point of interest among vegetarians, calling someone a "tofurkey" could be an insult in the same way it is to call someone a "turkey." However, more than likely it just means the person doing the name-calling is drunk and slurring his words.

Over the last few years, both tofu and tofurkey have become more and more popular among vegetarians, and people born without taste buds. However it still may take some time for these foods to catch on with the general public.

Until then, the next time someone teases you about your tofu, or being a vegetarian, just call them a tofurkey. Or wish them a bad case of the toe flu.

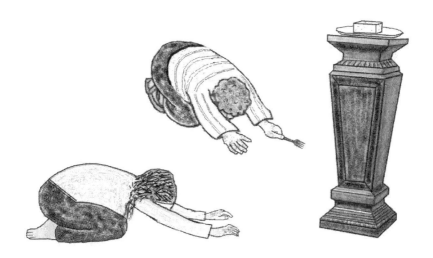

The Veggie Diary

I persuaded my neighbor, Randy, to give up his barbeque ribs and White Castle burgers to become a vegetarian. It wasn't easy talking him into it, but after a recent health scare, he was completely onboard with cutting meat out of his diet.

I instructed Randy to keep a diary of his day-to-day progress and to let me review it every week, so I could offer encouragement and advice. With his permission, I have printed Randy's diary entries from his first week as a vegetarian.

Randy Buford

Sunday, May 13th 10:10 P.M.
It's the night before I start my vegetarian diet. I am psyched! I know this will be better for my health and maybe help me lose a few lbs. To remind me I'm now a vegetarian, I put post-it's everywhere that all say the same thing – Do Not Eat Meat – Or I'll kick your ass! Of course I don't know how I would kick my own ass, but I'll worry about that later. I put the post-its everywhere I eat – on the fridge, on the kitchen table, on the toilet. So I am definitely ready. Had my last non-vegetarian meal today, a nice filet of cod

for dinner. Guess you could say I'm already a vegetarian since a lot of vegetarians eat seafood, right? But no seafood from here on. I'm doing this right. I'm going to avoid animal products altogether. So I guess technically I'm now a Veegun. So that's cool. Tomorrow I will be a new healthier person. I am psyched!

Sunday 11:35 P.M.
Just got back from White Castle. I'm not proud of myself. But technically my diet doesn't start until midnight. So no big deal. I just wanted to get a little taste of meat before I give it up forever. Besides I only had 2 hamburgers, even though I could have eaten more. So I definitely am exercising some willpower. Starting now I will be a vegetarian for life. This will be good. I am ready!

Monday, May 14th 8:40 P.M.
Excellent first day! No problem with breakfast. Had toast, OJ and Froot Loops as usual. But instead of milk, I had soy milk. It was a little weird, but OK. I can get used to it. For lunch I went out & got a Subway veggie sandwich. Made a veg stir fry for dinner. All went well w/no meat temptations. I feel healthier already. If I had known being a vegetarian would be this easy, I would have done it years ago.

Tuesday, May 15th 9:45 P.M.

Bit of a glitch this morning. After such a great day yesterday I guess I was over-confident, so I took down all the post-its last night. I figured I don't need no stinkin reminders. Well sure enough I got up this morning and completely forgot about the G-D diet. What an idiot! I was on auto pilot and just wasn't thinking. Made scrambled eggs and bacon like I have a thousand other times. Half way through the meal I realized my screw-up. Crap! I was doing so well too. It would have been wasteful to throw out the rest of my breakfast, so I ended up finishing it. Oh well, it was one minor 20 minute detour from my V diet. Besides a lot of vegetarians eat eggs, right? So technically I didn't really stray - except for the bacon. Anyway I threw out the rest of the eggs and there's no bacon left. So it won't be a problem going forward. The rest of the day went without a hitch. I feel good. I'm back in control.

Wednesday, May 16th 8:30 P.M.

A minor setback. The day started out well. I was back to Froot Loops for breakfast with soy milk. No problem. Lunch was a breeze -- tomato soup and PB&J sandwich at my desk. Then after work a few guys wanted to go out to O'Henry's to celebrate Roger's birthday from accounting. No problem. How could a couple drinks hurt? Well we had more than a couple drinks, it was getting late, and I was hungry. Someone ordered a couple plates of hot wings. I never told anyone I was a V, so it would have been weird to not eat any of them. Plus I was fucking starving. So I had one. Then another. Pretty soon I had wolfed down close to a dozen hot wings. Damn. It really felt like I screwed up. I should have just told everyone I was a V. But didn't want the questions. Then after I got home I started thinking. Maybe I didn't really screw up. Some vegetarians eat chicken, right? So maybe it wasn't so bad after all. I just strayed a little from my Veegun diet – but I'm still a V. It's not the end of the world. Anyway I'm now back on track. I feel positive. I can do better. Tomorrow will be a good day.

Thursday, May 17th 11:40 P.M.
Not a good day. Stressful as hell. Boss riding my ass about a stupid report I forgot to turn in. Screw him. What a jerk. He didn't need to make it into such a big deal. Coming home I instinctively pulled into White Castle. Can't say I didn't know what I was doing. I was hungry, stressed, didn't want to cook dinner. Just a small break from my V diet. Plus felt like a reward for putting up with all with this shit at work. Anyway I ended up gulping down 4 burgers. It <u>did</u> make me feel better. But felt guilty later. Oh well. I look at it this way – for this 24-hour day, I was a vegetarian for 23½ hours. That's like 99% of the time I was a V today. Not too shabby! Tomorrow will be even better. I WILL make it through tomorrow without eating any meat!

Friday, May 18th 10:45
Screwed up big time today! Whole day was a mess. It started with breakfast. Forgot to get groceries yesterday -- so out of Froot Loops. I was running late anyway, so decided to grab something at McD on way to work. Was just going to get a

danish & coffee but cute McD gal asked if I wanted to try egg McMuffin with sausage. Just said yes w/o thinking. Stupid idiot! After gulping that down I vowed to do better. But lunch was another disaster. It's Friday. We always go out as group. So where do they go today? Fucking Red Lobster! One of my favorites. Had to get Surf & Turf for old time's sake. OK 2 meals screwed up, vowed to do better at dinner. Again forgot to get groceries on way home. By the time I worked out and went out for groceries it was after 7. Didn't want to mess with making dinner. So made pit stop at Arby's. Figured I screwed up this day anyway, so what's one more meal with meat? No biggie. In my mind this day didn't count. Call it a mulligan in my V diet. A do over. I will get back on the V wagon tomorrow. Won't have the pressures of work on Saturday. It will be easy. I will be in complete control.

Saturday, May 19th 6:20 P.M.

Disaster of a day. Lost total control. Everything started out OK. Got up and went for a run, showered. Before I could fix breakfast got a call from my best bud Fred. He & guys were going out to breakfast at Denny's and invited me. I figured no problem. I could just order pancakes, which I love. So I get there and tell the guys I'm now a vegetarian and would appreciate their encouragement. Fat chance I'd get encouragement from these douchebags. They teased me, but I can handle it. But this was an impossible situation. All 3 of them ordered bacon with their breakfast. So when the food arrives, the waitress puts a big communal plate of bacon right in front me. Man it smelled good. I couldn't just sit there and stare at it, it was driving me crazy. Then Rex picked up a piece, started waving it around and held it under my nose. Not cool. So finally I gave in and helped myself to a couple of pieces. Besides it had been like FOREVER since I last had bacon. I guess since Tuesday. So breakfast is over, it's not even 10 A.M. and I've already screwed up. Damn it. I was so determined to do well today too. During breakfast Pete says the annual hotdog eating contest is this afternoon. I had forgotten all about it. A couple of years ago I was in it and did really well, came in 3rd & won $50. Again I told them that I'm a V now, so I can't eat hotdogs and shit like that. But they kept egging me on saying I could win the whole thing & $250 prize. I definitely could use the money. Then Fred says that if I eat a lot of hotdogs and then barf them all up it's like I never ate them at all. So I'm really not cheating at all on my V diet. That was an excellent point. The logic of his statement made complete sense to me at the time. Besides I had pre-registered for the contest a month ago. So to not do it was a wasted opportunity. The contest started at 3. I did well, but not as good as last time - finished 8th & out of the money. 34 hotdogs in 10 minutes. But felt bloated and sick afterwards. Never want to see another fucking hotdog as long as I live. After the contest I came home to take a nap, but decided not to barf up the hotdogs. That would have been gross. Maybe that contest is what I needed to get meat out of my system for good. I honestly feel like I am done eating meat for the rest of my life. The thought of it is just disgusting. And I am definitely done eating anything for the rest of day. Still feel stuffed.

Saturday 11:45 P.M.

Just got back from White Castle. This evening I was feeling better, and started to get hungry again. It was just too late to fix any kind of dinner - so went out for a couple of burgers. Not a big deal. Let's make this day another mulligan.

Sunday, May 20th 7:50 P.M.

No slip-ups at all today! -- if you don't count the pepperonis on the pizza that we had while watching the game. Besides that's a ridiculously tiny piece of meat. What is a pepperoni anyway? It's certainly not an animal. So is it really even meat? Not sure. But anyway I made it through my first week as a vegetarian. Not as hard as I thought it would be. I certainly wasn't perfect. I know I had a few slips. But if you look at the whole week I was probably off the V diet maybe 2% of the time. That means I was a vegetarian 98% of the time. So that's pretty damn good! But there's still room for improvement. Tomorrow I will do great!

Author's Note: After Randy gave me the first week of his diary to review, I told him he did very well and to keep up the good work. I also gave him some dietary tips.*

* *Truthfully I never actually read his diary. I was quite busy and Randy was bugging me for some feedback. So in a pinch, I gave Randy the same eating advice I give everyone: drink lots of water, chew slowly, and try not to spit food when you talk.*

Gift Buying for Vegetarians –
Dos and Don'ts

OK

Membership to "Fruit of the Month Club"

Not OK

Membership to "Liver of the Month Club"

OK

DVD "Meet Me in St. Louis" (1944 musical starring Judy Garland)

Not OK

DVD "Eat Me in Milwaukee" (1995 documentary of Jeffrey Dahmer)

OK

Gift certificate to Perkins Pancake House

Not OK

Gift certificate to Jimmy Dean's Slaughterhouse

OK

Rye Bread

Not OK

Rhino head

OK

Basket of Fudge Sauces

Not OK

Basket of Blood Sausage

Social Situations

A lot of social situations are challenging for vegetarians. You'll probably have to answer annoying questions about why you won't eat a "real" hamburger. You may need to fend off snide comments or cruel jokes about why you brought a cauliflower casserole to the potluck dinner. Or you may find yourself in a meat-meatless relationship, dating someone who eats cow's tongue and doesn't understand why you don't.

The social arena is a minefield of touchy situations which challenge your skill in tactfully dealing with people who are somewhat insensitive to the vegetarian mindset. The fact that these meat eaters haven't fully evolved, are completely ignorant, and morally inferior should not in any way cause you to think less of them.

So let's start with the social situations where you'll meet people who are interested in why you don't eat meat.

Common Questions

A lot of people will be curious why you don't eat meat. So be polite, friendly and succinct when you give your answers. Here's an example:

Question: Why don't you eat meat?

Incorrect **Answer:** Because I care about my health, animal welfare, and the environment, unlike you, you soulless Neanderthal.

Correct **Answer:** Because I've had Mad Cow Disease three times already and my doctor said if I get it again my brain will turn to oatmeal.

See the difference? The incorrect answer rambles with a few different reasons and might be construed as a bit condescending. The correct answer is to the point with a clear specific reason.

Here's another example of how to respond to a common question:

Question: Where do you get your protein?

Incorrect **Answer:** I get my protein from eating the hair stuck in my shower drain.

Correct **Answer:** I get protein mainly from nuts, beans, and chewing my toenails.

Notice the difference in tone? The incorrect answer is sarcastic, rude, and gross. The correct answer is straightforward, specific, and truthful.

Dealing with "Jokes" and Comments

Meat eaters sometimes think they're being funny when they say cruel things or make an attempt at humor with you being the butt of their joke. Be patient and forgive them for their insensitivity. You'll get your revenge later when you dance on their grave. Just kidding. You don't want to get dirt on your dancing shoes. You should accept their jokes with good spirit and respond when appropriate.

In fact, it's actually quite easy to deflect their joke with your own humorous comeback. Here's an example of how you can respond when confronted by a meat eater who makes light of your vegetarian diet.

> **Comment:** Vegetarians don't really live longer, it just seems that way. Ha Ha Ha
>
> *Incorrect* **Response:** That's a funny joke, Steve. Hey, didn't your father die of a heart attack from a clogged artery when he was 53?
>
> *Correct* **Response:** That's a funny joke, Steve. And speaking of life seeming longer, your life must seem *interminable*, being married to that nagging lard-ass.

See the difference? Both responses acknowledge the joke that Steve just made. However the incorrect response comments about Steve's father dying which is not all that funny. Whereas the correct response is humorous, teasing Steve back with a gentle zinger about his wife.

Dating

One of the challenges of the single vegetarian is finding compatible people to date. Fortunately in this high-tech age, there are several vegetarian online dating services which can help you find a compatible boyfriend or girlfriend. Or at the very least, these online services can validate your low self image as you get shot down as often online as you do in real life.

Here are a few dating services that I recommend:

VeggieShapeDate.com This creative dating service matches people by the "vegetable shape" of their body. For example, string-bean-bodied people are matched together as are avocado-shaped singles, pumpkin-shaped people, etc...

VeggieSex.com This a fun site for kinkier vegetarians who like to spice things up in the bedroom. Eschewing strawberries and whipped cream, they are more inclined to cover the bed with pickle relish, diced onions, and lima beans.

Veggistache.com This unusual dating site is for vegetarians with a fetish for moustaches. A bushy upper lip is a membership requirement for both men and women. Ironically women outnumber men on this site about 13 to 1.

HumptyDumptyDates.com This membership is specifically for ovo vegetarians who are accident prone.

VegVirgins.com. This club is for singles saving their first vegetarian meal for marriage.

VegomaticDate.com. This membership is for vegetarians guaranteed to sleep with you on the first date.

VERMIN.com. This online dating club is especially suited for athletic and uninhibited singles. It is open to vegans enjoying running marathons in the nude.

Dating a Meat Eater

No matter how hard you try to find a vegetarian soul mate, it's possible you may someday end up in a relationship with a non-vegetarian. Dating someone who does not share your vegetarian eating habits has a unique set of challenges.

Since so much about dating has to do with food and eating out, the differences between the two of you are often front and center on every date. For example, when you're at a restaurant and your date orders something you find a bit off-putting such as *walrus testicles*, what should you do?

Here are some options to consider:

A. Say nothing. Just grin and bear it.

B. Throw a hissy fit, then storm out of the restaurant.

C. Say nothing when she orders her meal but when it arrives, grab your date's plate, run to the restroom and flush the meal down the toilet.

D. Tactfully explain to your date that you are sensitive to certain foods being eaten in front of you and would prefer she order something else.

The correct answer is "C." When your date's plate arrives, grab it and run to the restroom to flush it down the toilet. For dramatic effect, when you grab the plate, you can yell something crazy like "THEY'RE TRYING TO POISON YOU!"

Your date will find you wild, impulsive and eccentric. And she will undoubtedly be even more attracted to you. If your date is overweight, she will also likely thank you for sparing her the calories and saturated fat.

Intimacy with a Meat Eater

Getting physical with a meat eater can be tricky. For example, if she's recently eaten a ham sandwich, you know she probably still has the dreaded "meat breath." Naturally you'll be quite reluctant to dive in for a passionate kiss. And no vegetarian would blame you.

Of course, you can ask your date to brush her teeth with Comet and gargle with rubbing alcohol. However, that might be considered rude and would probably break the romantic mood. A far better option is to slip on the *Kissing Condom*, pictured below.

With the Kissing Condom in place, the latex completely covers your mouth, so there is no chance of any meat molecules from your partner's mouth ending up in yours. There's even a tongue receptacle for French kissing. Your tongue is completely covered and protected should it make contact with your partner's tongue.

Your date will undoubtedly appreciate that you're prepared and taking precautions. You can now kiss with confidence, knowing that none of those tiny particles of meat in your date's mouth will cross over into yours.

The **Kissing Condom** gives you peace of mind when kissing a meat eater. It protects you from an unwelcome invasion of meat molecules from your partner's mouth.

Welcome back the
Vegetarian Olympics

Most non-meat eaters are excited at the recent announcement that the first modern Vegetarian Olympics will be held in Vegantown, Oregon in 2018.

The History

The ancient Vegetarian Olympics were last held over 3400 years ago. The Veggie Games, as they were known back then, took place in the small country of Vegistan in western Asia, in the region that is now part of Tajikistan.

Vegistan was a unique country in many ways. It was the only country in the history of civilization to outlaw the consumption of all animal products. Any Vegistanian found guilty of eating meat, drinking milk that came from an animal, or wearing fur or leather, was immediately banished from the country for life.

In ancient Vegistan, goats, sheep and oxen roamed the streets freely without fear, and even with a bit of cockiness. For awhile they even had equal protection under the laws established by King Tofutti III, who ruled Vegistan with both a hard fist and a soft heart for 43 years from 1483 B.C. until his death in 1440 B.C.

Unfortunately King Tofutti had to revoke his own law of equal protection just two years after implementing it. As it turned out, the chickens of Vegistan did not handle their freedom and idle time well. They caused a lot of mischief and ruffled quite a few feathers other than their own.

Conditions hit rock bottom in 1479 B.C. when several roving gangs of hens started a crime spree across the country, harassing and pecking people on the streets at night. For nearly two years these menacing gangs of chickens, nicknamed "The Mother Cluckers," terrorized communities after dark.

Finally something had to be done and King Tofutti amended his own law. Although consumption and use of animal products was still forbidden, nighttime curfews were implemented for all non-human residents of the country.

The nighttime animal curfews immediately helped reduce and eventually eliminate the crime sprees. From then on, Vegistan had very little internal strife and the animals and humans coexisted peacefully.

Of course, when the modern Vegetarian Olympics take place in a few years, there will be obvious changes to the structure of the games from ancient times. Back then only *male* humans, goats, sheep, yaks, pigs and roosters were allowed to compete. Also all participants competed completely naked, even the yaks. Finally, the loser of each event was beheaded in the town square the next day.

In the new modern Veggie Games, animals will not be competing. Only people will take part. However both men *and* *women* will participate. Clothing is strongly encouraged. And there will be no beheadings.

New Olympic Events

The modern Veggie Games will include the usual swimming and track & field events. However, with only vegetarian athletes competing, new events have been added which are more meaningful to the competitors. Here are three new events which are expected to be very popular.

- **Bean-Eating Contest.** This competition requires outstanding gastrointestinal fitness. The first contestant to finish one gallon of black beans is declared the gold medal winner. For their own respiratory safety, spectators are advised not to sit within 50 feet of the competitors.

- **Tofurkey Toss.** In this sport a 3-pound tofurkey is tossed by the women and a 5-pounder is thrown by the men. The participant with the longest toss is the winner and gets to take home his competitors' tofurkeys.

- **Hummus Wrestling.** The athletes do battle in a large tub filled with 500 gallons of hummus. The goal for the wrestlers is not to *pin* their opponents but to *dip* them. The first one to make a clean dip is the winner. Double dipping is not permitted.

Vegetarian Zodiac

Psychic-astrologer Patricia Van Winkle charts the horoscopes of vegetarians

Patricia Van Winkle is an experienced
astrologer, tarot-card reader
and whoopee-cushion tester.

Aries
March 21 - April 19

Your ruling vegetable: Rutabaga
Your birth bean: Garbanzo

Personality Traits & Predictions

You are optimistic. You expect that everyone you tell about your diet will immediately become vegetarian, only to realize that everyone you tell about your diet stops talking to you.

You are courageous. When in Los Angeles, you will lecture gangs of Crips and Bloods that they should become vegetarians, telling them it will be better for their health.

You are short-tempered. You will scold a waitress because your salad has a bacon bit. You will soon earn the nickname "Edgy Veggie."

Taurus
April 20 - May 20

Your ruling vegetable: Brussels Sprouts
Your birth bean: Pinto

Personality Traits & Predictions

You are patient. No matter how often you hear people mispronounce "quinoa," you refrain from ridiculing them.

You are stubborn. You will insist that God is an ovo vegetarian, despite the lack of solid evidence.

You are self-indulging. When given a gift certificate for dinner-for-two at your favorite vegetarian restaurant, instead of inviting a friend, you will go there alone and eat both dinners yourself.

Gemini
May 21 – June 20

Your ruling vegetable: Mustard Greens
Your birth bean: Jelly

Personality Traits & Predictions

You are witty. When you tell a funny joke at the vegan café, your friend will laugh so hard the soy milk comes out of her nose.

You are superficial. The main reason you pick up the new PETA magazine is because it features the world's sexiest vegetarians.

You are indecisive. When shopping at Walmart, you can't remember if you were supposed to get *bok choy* or a *boxed toy*, so you end up buying neither.

Cancer
June 21 - July 22

Your ruling vegetable: Texas Hairy Potato
Your birth bean: Cannellini

Personality Traits & Predictions

You are dependable. You will show up at an animal-rights protest despite not fully understanding the main message of the cause, "Rats are people too."

You are caring. You will gently catch a mosquito in your house, carefully put it in a jar, poke small air holes in the lid, and then drive it to the local wetlands preserve where you set it free.

You are adaptable. When you realize you're out of store-bought mushrooms, you will pluck the mushrooms growing from your living-room carpet and add them to your spaghetti sauce.

Leo
July 23 - August 22

Your ruling vegetable: Artichoke Hearts
Your birth bean: Kidney

Personality Traits & Predictions

You are melodramatic. At your favorite Italian restaurant, you will admonish the waiter that *you don't eat meat*, after you discover a severed finger in your minestrone.

You are ambitious. In your attempt to get into the *Guinness Book of World Records*, you will design plans to build the world's largest indoor tower made entirely of extra-firm tofu.

You are pretentious. Every chance you get, you will drop big words, like "probiotics" and "triglycerides," into casual conversations, even though you don't know their meaning.

Virgo
August 23- September 22

Your ruling vegetable: Pygmy Pumpkin
Your birth bean: Bladder

Personality Traits & Predictions

You are analytical. You will start counting the exact number grams of *each* of the 22 amino acids you intake each day and share this information on your Facebook page.

You are observant. When dining at a vegan café, you will notice the man seated at the next table is wearing a leather watchband, so you'll ask the manager to have him thrown out.

You are interfering. When a female friend starts dating a man who drives the Oscar Mayer Wiener-mobile, you hire a professional hit man to scare him to leave town before his wiener gets harmed.

Libra
September 23 - October 22

Your ruling vegetable: Schrute Beets
Your birth bean: Mexican Jumping

Personality Traits & Predictions

You are superficial. You will break up with your significant other, when you notice at a party that they have a big glob of baba ghanoush stuck in their hair.

You are observant. You will notice that a friend, who claims to be vegetarian, has the subtle scent of A-1 Sauce.

You are unreliable. You will pass up the anti-fur protest in order to attend a Cher concert.

Scorpio
October 23 - November 21

Your ruling vegetable: Monkey-Butt Squash
Your birth bean: String

Personality Traits & Predictions

You are passionate. You harshly scold your friend for being insensitive to vegetarians when she eats some Animal Crackers in front of you.

You are hospitable. You will let a family of gypsies live in your garage, after you hear the mother say that she once put a curse on Colonel Sanders.

You are jealous. When a friend's vegetable lo mein is clearly superior to your own recipe, you secretly wish that a big hunk of space debris will fall on her house.

Sagittarius
November 22 - December 21

Your ruling vegetable: Louisiana Stinky Cabbage
Your birth bean: Baked

Personality Traits & Predictions

You are adventurous. You will join the protest in Washington D.C. for equal rights for vegetarians, not fully understanding what that means.

You are kind. You will open your home to foster children, taking in orphaned vegetarians who were put up for adoption by their meat-eating parents.

You are humorous. When visiting Colorado, you will suggest to your pesco-vegetarian friend he should try the "Rocky Mountain oysters" since seafood is OK.

Capricorn
December 22 – January 19

Your ruling vegetable: Yolkless Eggplant
Your birth bean: Elle Elle

Personality Traits & Predictions

You are responsible. Before you serve the spaghetti to your dinner guests, you caution them that you accidently sneezed in the marinara sauce.

You are inhibited. You won't ever eat corn on the cob for fear of corn sticking in your teeth. Even when eating alone at home.

You are wary. At the health food store you can't decide whether to buy the *pea* protein, paralyzed by the irrational fear that it may in fact be *pee* protein.

Aquarius
January 20 - February 18

Your ruling vegetable: Dingleberry Peas
Your birth bean: Orson

Personality Traits & Predictions

You are clever. After having a Naked® fruit smoothie on the way to work, you tell your co-workers that you were just in your car drinking Naked. No one will seem surprised.

You are humanitarian. You will save a family of worms from drowning on the pavement after a heavy rainstorm, giving them a dry home in your largest potted plant.

You are unemotional. On the drive home, when you see roadkill, you do not get upset, mainly because it's a construction worker, not an animal.

Pisces
February 19 - March 20

Your ruling vegetable: Jumbo Julius Peppers
Your birth bean: Cloud Gate

Personality Traits & Predictions

You are imaginative. For Halloween you will dress up as a giant cube of tofu, but everyone will wonder why you're dressed as a "big white box."

You are accepting. When you learn that a friend doesn't feed his dog vegetarian dog food, you break off all contact with him, but still remain friends with his dog.

You are devoted. Following him from city to city, you will attend all the lectures of your favorite vegetarian author, until he gets a restraining order.

The Veggie Rap

Vegetables have long been much maligned. They are the second-class citizens of the dinner plate. Often relegated to side dishes, they are the bridesmaids at the meat's wedding. Even their first-cousin *fruit* is much more loved and appreciated. Vegetables are indeed the Rodney Dangerfield of food groups.

Here are 7 possible explanations why vegetables get no respect.

1. When growing up, children are told by their parents to eat their vegetables. When parents want you do something, it makes it inherently *uncool*.

2. When someone loses all brain activity but continues to breathe, they are referred to as being in a *vegetative state*. Or often they are called a *vegetable*. This comparison is not particularly flattering to vegetables.

3. The term "vegging out" is derogatory since it refers to not doing anything productive.

4. President George H. W. Bush publicly voiced his disgust for eating broccoli. In a memorable line from his 1990 State of the Union address he exclaimed "Read my lips. No more broccoli." Across America children cheered.

5. Compare the pronunciation of the word "veg-e-ta-ble" with the word "meat." Vegetable has many

more syllables and is harder to pronounce correctly. Consequently small children, people who stutter, and drunks will all avoid ordering vegetables.

6. Many vegetable-related terms are quite disparaging such as "corny," "cornball," "pea brain," " bean counter," "couch potato," "onion breath," and "zucchini nose."

7. Comedian *Carrot Top*. Enough said.

Despite the longstanding negative associations, there is some good news. A new political party is pushing to elevate vegetables to their rightful place in our diets and to give them the acclaim they deserve. And no, it's *not* the Green Party.

Rise of the Vegocrats

A new political party has recently risen from the growing vegetarian movement.

The fledgling **Vegocratic Party** has few members, little money, and no organization. What's more, they have virtually no name recognition.

And those are their *good* traits.

You see, the Vegocrats are a clean slate. There's nothing to trip them at the starting line. There have been no shady political contributions, no congressional page sex scandals, and no broken campaign promises. In other words, they don't have any of the baggage of the Democrats and Republicans.

They also have a platform of interesting, very progressive, and some would say wacky ideas, which should get vegetarian voters excited. In fact, they have already begun planning a run for the presidency in 2016.

In the process, the Vegocrats have nominated **Dr. Roscoe "Beanie" McBride** to head the party ticket. Dr. McBride is a charismatic figure who is sure to captivate vegetarians, vegans, and people named Beanie.

Here are some of the highlights of Dr. McBride's campaign platform:

- Outlaw the exploitation of helpless animals in circuses, in rodeos, and in family photos where they have to wear silly costumes

- Ban genetic engineering of *everything,* including animals, vegetables, and celebrity babies

- Offer tax exemptions to consumers buying food dehydrators, pleather, and Dr. McBride's autobiography

- Give education grants for studying: *The Evolution of the Cucumber*, *The Meat-Mafia Connection*, and *The History of the Vegocratic Party*

- Propose a constitutional amendment to make cauliflower the national flower

Roscoe "Beanie" McBride

Dr. Roscoe "Beanie" McBride has been a vegan his entire life. In fact, as an infant, he rejected his mother's breast milk in favor of a soy-based formula. In the 4ᵗʰ grade, McBride organized a successful boycott of the school cafeteria in order to get them to offer Veggie Sloppy Joes. In college he led an archaeologist expedition to the site of ancient Vegistan (in present-day Tajikistan), where his group discovered the precise location of King Tofutti's personal salad bar. He is a former two-term congressman from Mississippi.

Roscoe McBride was nicknamed "Beanie" by his parents because of his very large misshaped head that resembled a giant kidney bean. When he was 13 years old he had cranial surgery to correct the deformity, giving his head a less bean-like shape. But McBride could never shake the nickname.

Along with his sensible proposals, Dr. McBride has ideas that some consider radical. Here are a few of his more controversial promises:

- Change "In God We Trust" to "In Broccoli We Trust" on all U.S. currency.

- Ban the sale of the sugary fried-dough treat "Elephants Ears" because they're offensive to pachyderms and people with big ears.

- Rename sports teams, changing from names of carnivores to names of herbivores. Here are a few examples:

    - Chicago Bears would become the Chicago Hippopotamuses

    - Detroit Tigers would become the Detroit Chipmunks

    - Atlanta Hawks would become the Atlanta Manatees

- Switch pictures on money from presidents to famous vegetarians (For example, a $1 bill would have a picture of Jerry Garcia, a $5 bill would show Mr. Rogers, and a $10 bill would picture Lisa Simpson).

- Change the name of the state of Virginia to "Vegginia," and rename West Virginia "North Mississippi."

- Pay reparations to all Vegetarian-Americans in the amount of 40 mangos and a juicer.

What is Your V.Q.?

Discover Your "Veggie Quotient" with this Educational Quiz

The answers are on page 96

1. Which one of the following is technically *not* a vegetable?

   a. Asparagus
   b. Tomato
   c. Spinach
   d. Volkswagen

2. Which has the *most* fiber per 8-ounce serving?

   a. Romaine lettuce
   b. Bran flakes
   c. Prunes
   d. Tree bark

3. Which one of the following would make a good name for a band?

   a. Red Hot Chili Peppers
   b. Black Eyed Peas
   c. Strawberry Alarm Clock
   d. Edward Sharpe and the Magnetic Zucchini

4. Which of the following is *not* some type of bean?

   a. Red
   b. Black
   c. Pink Slime
   d. Rowan Atkinson

5. In ancient Vegistan, how many wives did King Tofutti III have?

   a. 1
   b. 2
   c. 147
   d. None, he was gay

6. In my neighbor Randy's first week as a vegetarian, how many trips did he make to White Castle?

   a. 1
   b. 2
   c. 3
   d. 11

7. What is the best way to cook vegetables so you preserve the most vitamins?

   a. Microwave
   b. Steam
   c. Bake
   d. Open car hood and place on top of engine

8. Which one of the following is the biggest nut?

   a. Hazelnut
   b. Peanut
   c. Brazil nut
   d. Charlie Sheen

9. Which group acts the *most* morally superior?

   a. Vegans
   b. Christian Conservatives
   c. Ex-Smokers
   d. Boy Scouts

10. If elected president, which one of the following actions has Roscoe "Beanie" McBride *not* promised to take?

    a. Declare the day after Presidents' Day "Tofu Tuesday."
    b. Mandate therapy to turn Angry Birds into mellow birds
    c. Erect a monument to Planters' Mr. Peanut
    d. Serve fruit-bean-pickle-and-ice-cube salad at his inauguration dinner

11. Which of the following is the *best* reason to *not* eat meat?

    a. Health
    b. Animals
    c. Environment
    d. Beef-Juice Stains

12. Which one of the following is *not* a vegetarian-friendly movie?

    a. Babe
    b. Chicken Run
    c. Fast Food Nation
    d. Milk

13. Which one of the following jobs has psychic-astrologer Patricia Van Winkle *not* done in the last 10 years?

    a. Fortune Teller
    b. Ghost Hunter
    c. Animal Communicator
    d. Hair Stylist to Donald Trump

14. If you get a *brain freeze* while drinking a raspberry smoothie, it's best to immediately do which of the following?

    a. Go the emergency room
    b. Enjoy feeling like Rick Perry for a minute
    c. Sue the establishment that sold you the smoothie
    d. Buy another smoothie in an effort to freeze another part of your body

15. What is gluten?

    a. Someone who eats to excess
    b. The "maximus" muscle of the buttocks
    c. A protein found in wheat
    d. When followed by "tag" means "Bite me" in German

16. Which one of the following eats eggs?

    a. Oboe vegetarian
    b. Volvo vegetarian
    c. Hobo vegetarian
    d. An omelet eater

17. Which is the *funniest* name for a fruit?

    a. Kiwi
    b. Honeydew
    c. Kumquat
    d. Ralph

18. Which one of the following can cause your brain to turn spongy and porous?

    a. Sad Cow Disease
    b. Mad Cowlick Disease
    c. Macaw Disease
    d. Eating at Arby's

19. Which one of the following cities was *not* considered as a site for the 2018 Vegetarian Olympics?

    a. Pyongyang, North Korea
    b. Tehran, Iran
    c. Mogadishu, Somalia
    d. Amarillo, Texas

20. Which one of the following would do the most damage to a parked car when dropped from the roof of a four-story building?

    a. 20 lbs. of blueberries
    b. 20 lbs. of tofu
    c. A 20 lb. watermelon
    d. Einstein's brain

Scoring

Give yourself one point for each correct answer.

1. b. A *tomato* is technically a *fruit*, not a vegetable. Go figure. We'll also accept **d.** Volkswagen. **2.** Unfortunately my assistant Sheldon did not get around to researching the answer, so give yourself one point no matter what you answered. **3. d.** This music question was a bit too obvious. **4. c.** No one knows what's in the beef-filler "Pink Slime," but chances are there are no beans. **5. c.** King Tofutti III had 147 wives and 963 offspring. That's why 3400 years later it's been said that everybody has a little Tofutti in their DNA. **6. d.** My neighbor Randy made 11 trips to White Castle during his first week as a vegetarian, eight trips which he failed to record in the Veggie Diary. **7.** Again Sheldon never got around to researching the answer. So give yourself one point no matter what you answered. **8. c.** In the Amazon, Brazil Nuts can grow up to 200 lbs., 30 lbs. more than Charlie Sheen. **9. d.** Those smug little Boy Scouts think they're so morally superior because they "help" people.

10. a. Roscoe "Beanie" McBride wants to declare the first day after *Labor Day* "Tofu Tuesday." **11. b**. Animal welfare is the best reason to become a vegetarian. **12. d**. Unlike its sequel "Soy Milk," the movie "Milk" does *not* promote vegetarianism. **13. b**. Patricia Van Winkle has never been a ghost hunter. **14. b**. Enjoy the moment. **15.** Once more Sheldon did not get around to researching the answer. Give yourself one point. **16. c**. Sometimes hobo vegetarians will fry up eggs in their boxcar. **17. c**. You can't beat "Kumquat" as a funny name for a fruit, family pet, or private body part. **18.** None of the above. Give yourself one point if you didn't answer the question. **19. d**. Amarillo, Texas was never considered for the Veggie Olympics for safety reasons. **20.** Unfortunately Sheldon was arrested before he could closely assess the damage to parked cars. Give yourself 5 points if you've ever tried this experiment yourself.

How did you do?

15 – 20+ Points. You rock! If you're not vegan, you're near-vegan

10 - 14 Points. Not bad. Keep eating those veggies!

5 - 9 Points. Work is needed here. Please go to the closest farmers market today, reread this book and order five more copies for friends.

0 - 4 Points. Oh my, this is serious!! If your arteries have not completely closed up yet, they will by tonight. Immediately order 100 more copies of this book to bequeath to friends and family.

A Look Ahead

So what's the future of vegetarianism?

Will the movement continue to grow? Will animal-rights issues become important to more people? Will we ever learn the correct pronunciation of *seitan*?

Since I'm not good at making predictions, I needed some help from a wise source with psychic insight. With my Magic 8 Ball broken, I once again called on my colleague Patricia Van Winkle.

I asked Patricia to peer into the future and tell me what the outlook was for vegetarianism.

For several seconds she gazed deep into her crystal ball. Then she told me something I did not want to hear, some bad news indeed. I had to pay her more money.

After I had written her a check and made her promise not to cash it until the end of the month, she stared again at her globe and began foretelling some very significant events.

On the next few pages, I've listed some of her more interesting predictions for the twenty-first century. She even told me who would be Time magazine's next "Person of the Year." (Spoiler alert: It's a popular cast member of Jersey Shore whose name rhymes with "rookie").

Patricia also revealed the surprising winner of the 2017 Super Bowl. Who knew *Fargo* would even get an NFL team?

And who would have guessed that Burger King would someday change its name to *Boca Burger King*? Or McDonald's best selling product would be the *McTofu*?

After hearing all of Patricia's predictions, it appears the future is very good for vegetarianism. And apparently also for Snooki.

Patricia Van Winkle is a
soothsayer, mind reader, and
licensed Zamboni driver.

Patricia's Predictions

November, 2016. Dr. Roscoe "Beanie" McBride will lose his independent bid for the presidency in a very close contest. Vegocrat McBride will split the liberal vote with Democrat Dennis Kucinich allowing Sarah Palin to win the election.

2017 – 2018. The Palin presidency will mark a dark time for animal rights as moose hunting will soar in popularity becoming the third most popular sport in America after NASCAR and snowmobiling. To the scorn of the "lamestream" media, Palin will even hold organized moose hunts on the White House lawn.

May, 2017. President Palin will order the removal of the vegetable garden planted by Michelle Obama and have it replaced with a turkey processing facility.

June, 2018. Sarah Palin suddenly and unexpectedly will quit the presidency announcing that she can better serve the country as a highly paid Fox News pundit. Vice President Gingrich will be sworn in as the 46th president. Wasting no time, Gingrich will immediately begin plans to add his face to Mt. Rushmore.

August, 2018. The Vegetarian Olympics will take place in Vegantown, Oregon, and be widely considered a success, with just a couple of glitches. One of the Kenyan marathoners will be arrested trying to sneak hyena meat into the Olympic Village. He will escape running down the Oregon coast barefoot, making it all the way to San Francisco before being arrested again. Also an errant tofurkey toss will hit an athlete from Kyrgyzstan, knocking him unconscious. However, he will fully recover.

May, 2020. Newt Gingrich will deliver on his eight-year-old promise to colonize the moon. To no one's surprise, the first building erected on the lunar surface will be a Starbucks.

November, 2032. In his third run for the presidency, Roscoe "Beanie" McBride will win in a very close election running against 97-year old Ron Paul, who will run for president for the fifteenth time.

2033 – 2040. President McBride will be continually frustrated by a Republican-controlled congress which refuses to enact any of his animal-rights legislation. Even his proposal to Congress to make it illegal to waterboard puppies will be soundly rejected.

2033. In his one major accomplishment in office, McBride will add a cabinet post for the Department of Animal Rights. He will appoint former parody musician Al Yankovic to the position of secretary. Many will call Yankovic a weird appointment.

2041. Despite his humiliating intern sex scandal of 2039, McBride will leave the presidency at the end of his eight-year term widely respected.

2057. The tide will turn for vegetarians and the animal rights community, as a majority of registered voters now identify themselves as Vegocrats.

2061. After some remodeling, all 1200 Outback Steak Houses will reopen as vegan cafes.

2064. As the memory of his grandfather has long faded from the minds of voters, Vegocrat George W. Bush III will be elected president. With a Vegocratically controlled congress, Bush will enact far-reaching animal-rights legislation, including outlawing factory farms, fur products, and *Itchy & Scratchy* cartoons.

2066. In the 100th Super Bowl, the Montpelier Maple Syrups will defeat the Honolulu Coconuts 30 - 28 on a last-second field goal by Betty Lu Groza. At the 84 NFL stadiums across the country veggie dogs will outsell meat hotdogs by 15 to 1.

2076. On the country's tri-centennial 73% of registered voters will identify themselves as Vegocrats. Eating meat will be considered as *stupid* and *uncool* as spitting on the living room carpet. Or listening to old recordings of Rush Limbaugh.

2082. Thirty years after his death, Roscoe "Beanie" McBride will replace George Washington on the one-dollar bill. Roscoe McBride Jr. will be present at the ceremony. However it will be a bittersweet occasion, as the one-dollar bill is virtually worthless. It now takes $300 just to buy a pack of gum.

2093. In an ironic twist of fate, one of the last known meat eaters in the country, Lester Thompson Jr., will be trampled to death by a herd of feral cows.

2100. In a poll of prominent historians, George W. Bush III will be rated as America's greatest president. Abraham Lincoln will come in a distant second. Sasha Obama will be third.

2107. A government spokesperson will announce that there are no longer any meat eaters living in the country. The U.S. is now officially a 100% vegetarian society. Somewhere Beanie McBride will be smiling.

About the Authors

Jim Tilberry has been a vegetarian since 1998. <u>Revenge of the Vegetarian</u> is his first attempt to write anything longer than a grocery list. He lives and works near Chicago. You can reach him at VeggieBook@aol.com.

Patricia Van Winkle has written 23 books on psychic matters, none of which have ever been published. She lives and works near Sedona, Arizona. If you wish to reach Patricia she will sense it and contact you.

Jim Tilberry's second book is <u>Coffee Dates From Hell</u>. This wacky work of fiction tells stories of hilariously awkward first dates, including coffee dates of Abraham Lincoln, Albert Einstein, J. Edgar Hoover and many others. This funny book is available online. Read more about it at www.CoffeeDatesFromHell.com.

Printed in Great Britain
by Amazon